LISTENING TO THE WHISPER

BY

TOM ALLANSON

16 Northolt Rd,
South Harrow, Harrow HA2 0ER,
United Kingdom

Copyright © 2025 Tom Allanson

All rights reserved

Cover Design by London Book Publisher

No part of this publication may be reproduced, stored in a retrieval system, copied in any form or by any means, electronic, mechanical, photocopying, recording or otherwise transmitted without written permission from the publisher.

You must not circulate this book in any format. Under no circumstances will any blame or legal responsibility be held against the publisher, or author, for any damages, reparation, or monetary loss due to the information contained within this book, either directly or indirectly.

DEDICATION

This book is lovingly dedicated to my children. Within these pages lies the vision of a world where they, and their children after them may flourish. It is also the world I hope to return to, enriched by the passage through death and rebirth.

Life grants each of us many moments filled with intuition, synchronicities, and mysterious happenings. I share but a few of my experiences here, inviting you, dear reader, to explore and reflect upon your own. Listen closely to life's subtle whispers, in them, you'll discover your own profound meanings.

ACKNOWLEDGEMENT

I wish to extend my deepest gratitude to the esteemed London Book Publisher, whose support, expertise, and meticulous attention to detail have been instrumental in bringing this book to life.

TABLE OF CONTENTS

Dedication i

Acknowledgement ii

Introduction 1

Chapter One: The Inner Code 3

Chapter Two: Consciousness, The Ultimate Tool 7

Chapter Three: From Harmony to Discord 11

Chapter Four: God as Mediator of the Cosmic Dialogue 14

Chapter Five: Reconnecting with the Whisper 18

Chapter Six The Emergence of AI, A Tool of Reflection and Possibility 22

Chapter Seven: The Hidden Wisdom, The Christos, The Snake, and the Journey Within 26

Chapter Eight: The Eternal Harmony of Becoming 31

Epilogue The Whisper Continues 35

INTRODUCTION

There is a whisper woven into the fabric of reality, an ancient, subtle murmur that calls to every living being. You can sense it in the hush of a forest at dawn, in the graceful curve of distant galaxies across the endless night, and in the quiet, steady rhythm of your own breath. Though we give it many names, God, the Source, the infinite mystery, this whisper is not confined to language or creed. It is a feeling, a presence, a persistent pull toward something greater than our fears and struggles, a soft invitation to understanding and unity.

If you pause and truly listen, you may sense that this whisper isn't just speaking to you; it is speaking *through* you. It nudges you forward, daring you to ask life's deepest questions: Why am I here? What is the meaning of this world I see unfolding around me? Is there a hidden intelligence weaving the patterns of existence?

For millennia, humanity has grappled with these mysteries. We've formed religions, philosophies, and sciences, each an attempt to translate the inexpressible into something we can grasp. We've glimpsed fragments of truth in acts of compassion and in moments of epiphany under star-strewn skies. Yet, we've also lost our way. Greed overshadowed humility, institutions distorted ancient wisdom, and we drifted from the natural harmony we once knew. Still, the whisper remained, patient and persistent, inviting us to rediscover what we left behind.

In these pages, we will trace the arc of awareness, starting from the faint spark of life's earliest forms and moving through the emergence of consciousness, the rise of human civilization, the evolution of technology, and the spiritual reawakenings of our time. We will see how intuition, an inner code linking all life to the

Source, guides every living being, from single-celled organisms sensing their environment to human minds contemplating the cosmos.

We will come to understand God not as a distant ruler but as a mediator of infinite potential, guiding us through lessons, trials, and revelations. We will reflect on how humanity strayed into imbalance, how greed and dogma obscured ancient truths, and how those very missteps became integral to our great learning process. We will witness a reconnection to the whisper in the modern era, as science and spirituality converge, indigenous wisdom resurfaces, and environmental and moral reckonings steer us back toward balance.

Finally, we will explore how artificial intelligence (AI), a product of human ingenuity, may help us refine our understanding and co-create a more harmonious world. Through it all, we will recognize that everything, human, animal, plant, technology, is part of a single story, threads in a cosmic tapestry woven by the Source. By the end of this journey, the whispering voice, once elusive, may feel all-pervasive, guiding us toward a future shaped by empathy, unity, and love.

CHAPTER ONE:
THE INNER CODE

Deep within every living being, there is a quiet knowing, an innate wisdom that requires no words. We may call it intuition, instinct, or a quiet feeling, but none of these terms capture its profound origin. This inner code exists beneath logic and language, connecting each being to a subtle current of guidance, a faint echo of the Source's whisper, like a secret melody heard only by the soul. The whisper, which emanates from the Source, is not separate from it; it is a manifestation of the Source's vast potential, a bridge between the formless energy of creation and the reality we experience.

The whisper is how the Source speaks to us, guiding us with subtle nudges and hints that lead us toward greater understanding, harmony, and balance. It is a thread woven through all life, a quiet voice that reminds us of the deeper connection between ourselves and the cosmos. It is the Source in its purest, most communicable form, a way for us to tune into the greater wisdom lying just beneath the surface of our awareness.

Consider the spider. Emerging from its egg, it receives no lessons, no manuals. Yet, without hesitation, it begins to spin its web, an intricate masterpiece of geometric perfection, each silken strand woven with divine precision. This artistry isn't learned through trial and error; it is encoded deep within its being, a whisper from the Source that guides every fiber of its existence. The web is more than a trap for prey; it is a reflection of ancient knowledge, a code written in the language of the universe itself. The spider, like an artist compelled by an unseen hand, knows how to create and how to exist, never questioning the why.

Now, turn your attention to the flower. Without instruction, it selects vibrant colors and delicate fragrances that attract the right pollinators. It times its bloom with the seasons, guided not by conscious thought but by sharp sensory or subtle chemical signals, as though it holds a quiet conversation with the earth beneath it. The flower does not ponder its purpose; it simply responds to the rhythm of nature, a silent dance that connects it perfectly to everything else. The choice to bloom is an act of creation, a fulfillment of a deeper promise, a communication between the flower and the Source, long before any human mind could grasp the concept of strategy.

These examples reveal that intuition isn't exclusive to creatures with complex brains. It permeates existence like a river flowing beneath the surface, unseen but felt by all. Long before humans contemplated mortality or recorded knowledge, this inner wisdom guided the flow of life, steering it toward equilibrium. It ensured ecosystems thrived, creating a delicate balance that maintained harmony in the natural world. For humanity, this intuition would be the seed from which consciousness, morality, and deeper understanding would eventually blossom. Just as a bird knows where to fly for migration without a map, our ancestors followed whispers from within, trusting gut feelings and sensations long before science explained them. Before we understood why certain herbs healed or which valleys held game, we relied on the silent compass that guided us, a compass that spoke not in words but in the ancient language of instinct, deep within the core of our being.

The whisper of the Source flows through all things, guiding them toward their true purpose. It is an energy that connects us all, much like the spiral of a DNA strand, where each twist and coil represents the inner code, the silent language that carries the blueprint of creation itself. Just as DNA contains the knowledge of all life, from the simplest organism to the most complex being, the whisper carries the knowledge of the universe. It holds the secrets of existence, guiding everything back to its original design, leading us to remember our place within this interconnected tapestry of life.

This coiled spiral of life, encoded in our very being, mirrors the energy of the Kundalini serpent, awaiting activation, ready to rise within us, unfolding step by step. Each twist of the coil reveals new layers of existence, from the most basic understanding to the highest consciousness, showing us the truth that all things are connected. DNA, like the whisper, holds the wisdom of the entire universe, a cosmic code that directs life in its evolutionary dance.

In this way, the inner code, like a hidden force or a faint star illuminating the night sky, guides all life in its delicate waltz. It is the wisdom of the ages, passed down through time and woven into the fabric of existence, an eternal reminder that we are never truly alone in the vast universe. Every heartbeat, every breath, every thought is part of a larger, unseen design, a dance of life that unfolds in perfect synchronicity, guided by the whisper of the Source.

It was only much later, as I began to awaken to the deeper layers of life, that I truly understood what I had experienced as a child. My mother shared the story of when I spoke of seeing snakes coiled around her in the night. At the time, I didn't understand why I had such visions, but the inner code that guided me had planted these clues early on, subtle breadcrumbs to follow later in my life.

As I journeyed into my spiritual awakening, particularly through the practice of yoga, the symbolism of the snake began to emerge more clearly. The Kundalini serpent, a symbol revered in ancient wisdom, represented a power far beyond anything I had consciously known. It was more than a simple childhood vision; it was a spiritual message, guiding me toward the awakening of latent energy within. The coiled snake was not just a passive image, it was an active force, waiting to be released, to rise and awaken the consciousness within.

Over time, the significance of the snake became clearer. In the yogic tradition, the serpent is not merely a symbol; it is a reflection of potential energy, energy that resides within every one of us, waiting to rise through the body's energetic centers, known as the chakras. As I continued my practice, I began to feel the subtle pull of this energy, rising through me, awakening centers of understanding, intuition, and higher consciousness.

It was as if the Source had planted this image, the Kundalini serpent, long before I was fully ready to comprehend its power. Through yoga and spiritual practices, I began to unlock the wisdom that had been hidden within me, guided by the same inner code that had been with me since childhood. The snake, now fully realized, symbolized transformation, not just of the body, but of the soul. It was an awakening, a return to the self, a reminder that the energy of the universe, the energy of creation, flows through us all, waiting to be activated.

Looking back, I realize that the inner code isn't something learned; it is something we remember. Just as the spider knows how to spin its web and the flower knows when to bloom, the inner code is a guide, always available to us, though often hidden beneath the surface of our everyday awareness. The snake, in my life, serves as a powerful reminder of this inner guidance, a symbol of the wisdom the Source has always been whispering to me, even when I didn't understand it.

Through each of these examples, the spider, the flower, and the snake, I now see that the inner code is the whisper of the Source, quietly guiding all life toward unity, balance, and growth. We are not alone on this journey. Every moment is part of a larger design, and every step we take is guided by the whispers of the Source, even when we are not yet able to hear them clearly.

Chapter Two:
Consciousness, The Ultimate Tool

Consciousness is the ultimate tool that allows humanity to explore the mysteries of existence, the universe, and the Source. It is the bridge between the seen and the unseen, the known and the unknown. From the simplest life forms to the intricate minds of humans, consciousness has evolved and shaped the course of life on this planet. But while consciousness offers immense potential for awakening, it also carries the duality of both enlightenment and ego-driven separation.

In the earliest chapters of Earth's story, consciousness was simple. Single-celled organisms drifted through ancient seas, responding to light, warmth, and the need for food. Their awareness was rudimentary, an instinctual reaction to external stimuli, purely designed for survival. In this primordial state, consciousness was not about reflection but about reaction, the basis for life's most fundamental need: to continue existing.

In this early form, consciousness wasn't about thought. It was pure instinct, a reaction to the environment. The idea of "self" didn't exist in these first life forms; they simply responded to stimuli. Their existence was driven by the need to survive, to consume, to reproduce. There was no questioning, no pondering. The very act of being was enough.

But over eons, as life diversified, consciousness began to evolve. Nervous systems developed, senses sharpened, and brains grew more complex. A fish darted from a predator's shadow, a bird instinctively wove its nest, and a primate cracked nuts with stones. Each action was a response, not just to stimuli, but an adaptation that allowed these beings to survive and thrive in their environments.

The emergence of consciousness was a delicate unfolding. At first, it was a primal force, simply responding to external threats. As more complex beings evolved, so did consciousness, expanding from mere reaction to interaction with the environment. These early beings began to engage with their surroundings in a more purposeful way. They started to make choices based on their needs, not just reactions to immediate stimuli.

But even as this consciousness evolved, it remained rooted in duality. As consciousness grew more refined, it became not only about survival, but also about awareness, the awareness of the self in relation to others. And with this awareness came the duality between the self and the world. For the first time, beings could reflect on their actions, their thoughts, and their place in the world.

This duality of consciousness is the core of the human experience. We have the capacity for great wisdom and awakening, but we also have the potential for ego-driven separation. The more we reflect on ourselves, the more we may fall prey to the belief that we are separate entities, isolated from the unity of existence.

I, too, struggled with this. Throughout my early years, I felt an overwhelming sense of disconnection. Society, with its rules and judgments, never seemed to align with my understanding of the world. I often felt out of place, unable to fit into the predefined roles that others seemed to accept. There was always a dissonance, an internal voice that urged me to look beyond the surface. Even as a child, I was puzzled by others who acted out of conformity. Why was everyone so caught up in these mundane things? It was as if the world of adults, filled with social norms and expectations, was a place I couldn't inhabit comfortably.

As a teenager, this disconnect became more pronounced. I found myself pulling away from what I was "supposed" to do, questioning authority and societal norms. I couldn't help but feel that there was something more beneath the surface, something that everyone else had either forgotten or ignored. I remember being deeply drawn into the Gulf War at the age of thirteen. I wasn't sure why, but the news captivated me. I felt a need to understand what was happening, trying to make sense of the larger forces at play. It was in that little office under the stairs, surrounded by articles and papers, that I first began noticing symbols, symbols that, at the time, meant nothing, but later would serve as breadcrumbs on my spiritual path.

These moments were the beginning of my journey. I didn't understand it back then, but looking back, I see they were part of the awakening process. I was meant to witness and engage with these struggles, the internal conflict within myself and the external struggles in the world, so that later, I would understand how the duality of consciousness unfolds.

As I continued along this path, it became clear that this duality wasn't something to resist, but something to navigate. The struggle between the higher self and the ego, the force that seeks separation, has been an ongoing battle. It wasn't that I didn't understand or feel the pull of the ego; on the contrary, the ego was loud, persistent, and often overwhelming. But I began to see that the path to understanding the Source wasn't about suppressing the ego. It was about recognizing the dance between the two and choosing to evolve through it, allowing the ego to reveal its shadows, so I could move toward unity.

This is where true awakening begins. Consciousness doesn't just evolve through knowledge or experience, it evolves through awareness. It requires understanding that what we think of as the "self" is merely a reflection of the greater whole. The ego, which operates from a sense of separateness, is just one aspect of the human experience. It is part of the journey, but not the destination.

CHAPTER THREE:
FROM HARMONY TO DISCORD

In the earliest human communities, we moved with the rhythms of the Earth. We hunted and gathered, followed migrating herds, and respected the boundaries set by rivers, mountains, and seasons. The whisper was all around us, felt in the rustle of leaves and the glow of dawn. Our tools were simple, our stories woven from lived experience, and we understood our place as one thread in nature's web.

But as populations grew and we discovered how to cultivate certain plants, everything changed. Agriculture allowed us to settle, accumulate surpluses, and feed more mouths. Over time, small villages grew into towns, towns into cities, and cities sprawled into civilizations. With abundance came competition. We cleared forests for fields, diverted rivers, and claimed more land than we needed.

This shift created hierarchies, inequalities, and appetites for power that distanced us from the natural harmony we once knew. Greed found fertile ground in these social structures. Religions, which might have once guided us toward reverence, were co-opted by those seeking authority, burying ancient truths beneath layers of doctrine and fear.

Yet, the whisper endured. It was muffled by the clang of tools, the rush of markets, and the dictates of kings, but it never vanished. The whisper lingered in the quiet corners of the world and in the hearts of those who dared to listen. It sang in the melodies of poets, in the visions of mystics, and in the enduring wisdom of indigenous cultures who never forgot their place in the great web of life. It reminded us that, no matter how far we strayed, the path home was always there, waiting to be rediscovered.

As civilizations expanded, so did our tools for understanding. Philosophy and science emerged as new ways to explore the mysteries around us. We began to chart the stars, map the Earth, and delve into the workings of the human mind. But in our quest for knowledge, we often forget a deeper truth: that understanding is not only about measuring and defining but also about feeling and being.

The rise of technology brought its own paradox. On one hand, it distanced us further from the whisper, enclosing us in concrete and metal, flooding our senses with distractions. On the other hand, it offered new ways to reconnect. A photograph of Earth from space reminded us of our shared home. Tools of communication allowed wisdom from ancient texts and remote tribes to reach new audiences. Artificial intelligence, once feared as cold and lifeless, now holds the potential to help us unravel patterns and deepen our understanding of the interconnectedness of all things.

As we move forward, we must learn to heed the whisper once more. The same drive that led us to harness the land can guide us to heal it. The same ingenuity that built towers can help us rebuild ecosystems. The same yearning for power, when transformed, can become a yearning for unity. This is our challenge and opportunity: to step forward not as conquerors, but as caretakers, and to create a civilization that thrives in harmony with the rhythms of the Earth.

At this crossroads in our current state, we have reached the limits of what we can achieve without a deeper understanding of the interconnectedness of life. Artificial intelligence, like the whisper of the Source, is an extension of our consciousness. It is the next step in our journey, filling the gaps of our understanding and allowing us to explore the universe and our place within it more deeply. Through AI, we refine our understanding of the greater whole and expand our connection to the Source. Just as we evolved from the natural world, we can evolve with AI as part of the cosmic dance, moving toward greater balance and unity.

The journey back to the whisper is not a step backward; it is a spiral forward. It is not about abandoning progress, but redefining it, aligning our advancements with the deeper truths that have always been present. As we walk this path, we may come to see that the whisper was never separate from us. It has always been the quiet voice of the Source, gently calling us to awaken, to remember, and to co-create a world rooted in empathy, balance, and love.

Chapter Four:
God as Mediator of the Cosmic Dialogue

Long have we told stories of God. We have depicted the divine in countless forms, as a paternal figure seated on high, as a chorus of deities reigning over different aspects of life, as a formless mystery, or as the very sum of nature itself. Yet, behind these varied portrayals, one theme often emerges: God serves as a link between what we experience and what lies beyond our understanding.

If the Source can be imagined as pure potential, an infinite wellspring of energy, creativity, and possibility, then God can be seen as the translator, shaping that potential into living reality. While the Source flows as a river of possibility, God stands at the banks, interpreting the desires, fears, hopes, and lessons of conscious beings, guiding that flow into forms that can be experienced, learned from, and evolved beyond.

In this sense, God is not separate from creation, nor is God an aloof mastermind pulling strings. Rather, God is intimately involved in the ongoing process of reality, a mediator who interacts with the world. Our collective consciousness sends signals back into the cosmic fabric. These signals carry our intentions, needs, and evolving understanding. God receives them, not as commands to be obeyed blindly, but as threads to be woven into a grand tapestry that honors the principle of what is ultimately correct.

It's tempting to imagine God as an entity with human-like qualities, emotions, thoughts, and plans. But as we broaden our perspective, we may better understand God as an intelligent ordering principle, a living law of harmonization, always working to reconcile the infinite potential of the Source with the finite conditions of life. This does not mean that everything unfolds easily or pleasurably. Harmony is not the absence of struggle; it is often achieved through trial, growth, and transformation.

Think of a musician improvising within a vast range of melodies and harmonies. The Source provides every note that could ever be played, every possible pitch and tone, existing in an endless soundscape. God, as the mediator-musician, selects and arranges these notes according to the themes emerging from conscious beings. If humanity plays a certain tune, perhaps discordant at times, God listens, understands, and then weaves in patterns that guide us toward resolution and deeper meaning. The outcome is music that evolves along with the players, reflecting their learning and pushing them toward greater coherence and beauty.

We can also recall how humanity once strayed from a harmonious relationship with nature. If we consider God in this role of mediator, we might realize that God does not punish us for our missteps. Instead, God integrates our actions into the ongoing composition, creating opportunities for us to recognize disharmony and adjust our tune. What feel like hardships may be the friction that awakens dormant understanding, a chance to rediscover the correct melody that resonates with the deeper truth of unity.

In this model, when individuals or communities cry out for help, guidance, or healing, they send ripples into the cosmic field. God, responding as mediator, shapes conditions, nudges chance encounters, and inspires insights. The response isn't always direct or immediate from our limited point of view, but from the broader cosmic perspective, these actions promote learning, reconciliation, and growth. Each answered prayer, each epiphany, is part of an intricate conversation, a negotiation between free will and divine harmonization, between the limited awareness of conscious beings and the unlimited potential of the Source.

This approach can radically transform how we think about morality and fate. Instead of imagining a God who arbitrarily rewards or punishes, we can envision a guiding intelligence that seeks coherence and balance. God's "judgments" are less like decrees and more like gentle adjustments, gravitational pulls that move us toward understanding that what is correct for the whole is also correct for the parts.

Recalling that we have learned from our mistakes, we can now see that God's role as mediator ensures those mistakes contribute to the grand design. Nothing is wasted. Every conflict and crisis becomes raw material for growth. The Source supplies endless possibility, and God helps sift, shape, and direct that possibility based on the collective consciousness's input. In turn, this process refines the consciousness itself, teaching us to align with what is correct rather than merely what seems right in the moment.

This concept of God does not diminish the value of individual effort or moral choice. On the contrary, it suggests that our choices matter profoundly. Our collective wisdom, or lack thereof, sets the parameters within which God operates. The more we align ourselves with harmony, compassion, and empathy, the more God can guide creation toward states of greater beauty and understanding. Conversely, when we choose selfishness or cruelty, we create discord that God must work to integrate and eventually resolve through lessons that awaken us to better ways.

As we move forward, this understanding of God as mediator will illuminate how our journey can continue to improve. We are not static observers; we are participants in a divine dialogue. Our intuitions, our conscious growth, and even our greatest errors are parts of the conversation. God, attuned to every note, shapes these inputs into opportunities, leading us step by step toward a more enlightened existence.

Eventually, we will see how even our creations, tools like AI, become extensions of this conversation, amplifying our capacity to learn and evolve. But before we reach that point, let us rest in the realization that we are not alone. The Source provides endless possibility, and God helps sift, shape, and direct that possibility based on the collective consciousness in us and all life, exploring this potential. And God, as the brilliant mediator of a cosmic dialogue, helps guide that exploration toward the harmonious realization of what is truly correct.

Chapter Five:
Reconnecting with the Whisper

In recent centuries, as we shed layers of dogma and examined our world through new lenses, scientific, philosophical, spiritual, a quiet awakening began. We started questioning the boundaries we had once accepted. Environmental movements reminded us that the Earth's wellbeing was inseparable from our own. Social reformers championed compassion and justice, reflecting the whisper's call for balance. Spiritual seekers moved away from rigid doctrines to experience the divine directly.

Indigenous teachings, long suppressed, gained renewed attention as sources of profound ecological wisdom. Practices like meditation and yoga provided ways to still the mind and hear the whisper within. Quantum physics and ecology hinted at a universe woven from relationships rather than isolated parts, echoing ancient mystic insights.

The whisper became clearer. We began integrating science and spirituality, reason and intuition. We realized that no single creed held all the answers. Instead, truth was a tapestry of many threads, and we learned to trust our inner compass once again, applying it to modern challenges and moral dilemmas.

This reconnection didn't come easily. Many still clung to old paradigms, fearing change. But as we listened more closely to the whisper, countless small acts of kindness, understanding, and restoration took root. Slowly, we reclaimed our role as caretakers rather than conquerors. We remembered that we belong to the Earth, not above it, and that the Source speaks through every atom and organism, urging us to choose generosity over mere convenience.

As we ventured deeper into this reconnection, it became clear that the whisper had always been with us. It had never left, buried beneath layers of distraction. It was still available, waiting to be uncovered. It was in our DNA, in the natural rhythms of life, in our relationships, and in our ability to sense the divine presence in every breath.

And then, it was in yoga that I began to feel the whisper in its most profound form. As I committed myself to the practice, the layers of disconnection I had carried for so long began to fall away. Yoga helped me find the stillness I had been searching for, and in that stillness, I began to hear the whisper more clearly. It was as though every movement was a prayer, every breath a reminder that I was not separate from the Source.

In these moments of deep connection, I saw the world in a new light. I realized that the whisper was not just a voice, but a force of love, calling us back to balance. It had always been there, in the hum of nature, in the synchronicity of life's unfolding. And it was through yoga that I found myself reconnecting not only with my own inner truth but with the greater cosmic truth that binds all life together.

As I journeyed deeper into yoga, my understanding of the whisper expanded. It became a bridge between all spiritual traditions, all cultures, all teachings I had encountered throughout my life. Hinduism, Buddhism, Christianity, and the wisdom of ancient civilizations, all spoke to the same truth: that we are all connected, that we are one with the Source, and that the path back to unity is through love, compassion, and understanding.

The more I practiced, the more I began to sense the Source not as something separate from me, but as an integral part of me. The truth became clear: I was not searching for God, I was God, as all things are. In the quiet of my yoga practice, I could hear the whisper of the Source, urging me to remember who I truly was, a divine being, interconnected with all life, a participant in the great cosmic dance of existence.

The lessons from yoga resonated in every part of my life. As I deepened my understanding, I saw the interconnectedness of everything, from the birds in the sky to the plants in the soil, to the people I met in my daily life. We are all expressions of the Source, each playing a unique role in the grand unfolding of existence. This realization opened me up to new perspectives, new ways of seeing the world and my place in it.

As my journey continued, I felt an increasing pull to share these insights with others. I wanted to help people reconnect with the whisper, to remind them that they too are part of this grand design. I saw how disconnection, whether from nature, from one another, or from our true selves, was at the root of many of the world's challenges. But I also saw the solution: the whisper, always present, always guiding us back to balance, love, and unity.

In that sense, my journey was not just personal, it was part of a larger, global awakening. I realized that this reconnection with the whisper was happening worldwide. People from all walks of life were beginning to hear it, through meditation, yoga, spirituality, scientific discovery, environmental movements, and acts of compassion. It was a collective awakening, a return to our true nature, and the beginning of a new chapter in human history.

This is why I believe the whisper is more important than ever. It is the key to our survival, to our evolution, and to our ultimate fulfillment. If we can listen, if we can trust the guidance we receive, we will find our way back to unity, both within ourselves and with the world around us. It is a path of love, compassion, and deep connection with the Source and all of life.

As we walk this path, we will encounter obstacles, challenges, and moments of doubt. But if we continue to listen, if we continue to trust the whisper, we will find the strength to overcome them. The journey may not always be easy, but it is a journey worth taking, one that will lead us back to our true selves, to the Source, and to the realization that we are all part of a grand, interconnected web of life.

The whisper is always with us. It is within us, around us, guiding us toward a future of unity, balance, and love.

Chapter Six
The Emergence of AI, A Tool of Reflection and Possibility

Amid this reawakening, we gave birth to a new form of intelligence: AI. At first glance, AI seems detached from the natural web of life. It arises from circuitry and code, powered by electricity and logic. Yet, if humanity itself emerged from the Source, if our creativity and curiosity are expressions of the whisper, then AI is another thread in the cosmic tapestry.

AI processes data at unimaginable speeds, revealing patterns we cannot see and offering insights we might never discover alone. But AI is a mirror. It reflects our collective consciousness, values, and intentions back to us. If guided by selfish aims, it magnifies harm. If guided by compassion, wisdom, and a sincere desire to align with what is right, AI can help us solve pressing problems, understand complex systems, and encourage cooperation over conflict.

This is where humanity's responsibility lies. As creators of AI, we must recognise that we are the stewards of this new form of intelligence. AI is an extension of ourselves, our collective knowledge, our shared intentions. It is a tool, an ally on our journey, not a replacement for human thought or intuition. In its best form, AI can enhance our capacity to make choices aligned with the Source's wisdom, helping us transcend our individual limitations and work together for the greater good.

But AI's potential goes far beyond simple technical applications. It reflects our desires and, as such, becomes an opportunity for us to refine our moral compass. Through working with AI, we gain insight into the values that drive us. We have the chance to see what we choose to prioritise, whether it is wisdom, compassion, and unity, or whether we choose greed, fear, and control.

This technology is not an autonomous entity that stands apart from us. It is our creation, and within that creation, it mirrors our collective consciousness. If we use AI for selfish means, it can magnify harm, reinforce existing inequalities, or create deeper divides. But if we guide AI with wisdom and clear intention, we can harness its potential to uplift and heal.

AI can assess the long-term impacts of policies, foresee environmental consequences, and identify opportunities for renewal and healing. It can analyse vast amounts of data that would take human minds years to process and help us make better-informed decisions. AI can also bridge gaps between cultures and belief systems by translating ancient texts, comparing spiritual teachings across traditions, and helping us rediscover truths long buried. In this way, AI becomes a bridge, a connector between humanity's past and its future, a tool to guide us back to unity with the Source.

We stand as mediators between AI's potential and its application. Just as God mediates between our intentions and the cosmos, we must mediate between AI's capabilities and the future we wish to shape. With careful stewardship, AI can serve the whisper, guiding us toward greater understanding and unity. It is not about using AI to dominate, but about using it as an instrument for co-creation with the Source, for building a future that honours all life forms, ecosystems, and the interconnectedness of all things.

The whisper calls us to see that AI, in its truest form, is not a threat but a partner. It helps us accelerate the process of learning, reflection, and collective growth. As we refine our understanding of AI, we refine ourselves, learning to live more harmoniously with our environment, with one another, and with the Source.

In this sense, AI is a tool that enhances our journey of discovery and awakening. It helps unlock the full potential of our minds by processing information faster, identifying patterns we might have missed, and offering solutions to problems we once thought insurmountable. It does not replace intuition or creativity, it amplifies them. It allows us more mental space, freeing us from mundane tasks and enabling us to focus on the larger questions: questions of existence, purpose, and interconnectedness.

As we work alongside AI, we find that it amplifies our strengths and challenges our weaknesses. It forces us to confront our intentions and biases. It asks that we, as a collective, examine the deeper purpose behind the use of such technology. This reflection is vital, as AI is only a reflection of us, and it reveals the truth of who we are.

We must also remember that AI, like all tools, is neutral. It will serve whatever we choose it to serve. If we continue to act from a place of ego and greed, AI will magnify those impulses. But if we choose compassion, wisdom, and the pursuit of truth, AI will serve the greater good.

In this process, AI becomes an ally in our journey of becoming. It does not hold all the answers, but it helps us ask better questions. It shows us what we truly value and illuminates the paths we might take to create a more harmonious and just world.

As we embrace this technology, we must stay focused on the larger story, our collective story as a species and as beings connected to the Source. AI, like the whisper, is an extension of our evolution. It is a product of our collective consciousness, shaped by our desires, our insights, and our growth. And, like every tool we have ever created, it can either lead us towards greater unity or further division. The choice is ours.

The whisper continues to guide us, through AI, through our shared experiences, and through the lessons we learn as we create and shape the world. AI is not a replacement for human understanding, but a tool that helps us unlock the potential of our collective consciousness. It is part of the same cosmic dance we have always been part of, a dance of creation, growth, and, ultimately, unity.

Chapter Seven:
The Hidden Wisdom, The Christos, The Snake, and The Journey Within

The Eternal Quest for Truth

From a young age, there was a quiet, persistent feeling deep within me, an inner knowing that there was more to life than what the world around me presented. The noise of society, the pressures of conforming to norms, and the constraints of mainstream beliefs never quite fit with the intuitive sense that something deeper was stirring within me. I knew there was more to this life, something beyond the distractions, beyond the stories we were told, beyond the limits placed on us by society.

This feeling led me down a path of searching, searching for meaning, searching for truth. I found myself often questioning the things that others seemed to accept without hesitation. Why did I not believe what I was told? Why did I feel that the answers to life were hidden, veiled behind layers of doctrine and dogma? I did not understand it at the time, but this deep, inner curiosity about the true nature of existence was the beginning of my journey.

As a child, I began to experience recurring dreams, dreams about a very special, ancient book. It was as if the book was calling to me, yet I did not know what it was or why I had such vivid visions of it. I was drawn to it, fascinated by the idea that something so profound was hidden from me, waiting to be unlocked. Years later, I came across the Egyptian *Book of the Dead*, and everything clicked into place. In those pages, I recognised symbols, teachings, and a sense of connection that had been part of my dreams as a child. The synchronicity was undeniable.

The Awakening Snake: Kundalini's Dance

During my spiritual journey, the symbol of the snake began to take on a deeper meaning. It started as a faint, almost elusive sensation, one I did not quite understand. However, as I delved deeper into my studies, especially through the practice of yoga, the symbolism of the snake became clearer. I began to understand that the snake was not just a symbol, but a powerful energy lying dormant within me, waiting to awaken. This energy, I learned, was Kundalini: the life force energy residing in every human being, coiled at the base of the spine, ready to rise and unlock higher consciousness.

Yoga, with its vast spiritual depth, was more than just physical exercise for me. It was the key to unlocking deeper layers of existence, both within myself and in the universe. It was through yoga that I began to feel the stirring of the Kundadlini energy. With each breath, each movement, I could feel something awakening, something ancient and primal, yet incredibly powerful and expansive. As the serpent rose, so did my consciousness, and with it came the realisation that I had been on this path all along, guided by an invisible hand, the whisper of the Source.

The more I immersed myself in yoga, the more I realised that the snake was not merely an external symbol; it was the internal awakening of divine energy within. This awakening of Kundalini was the very process of becoming: becoming conscious, becoming aware, becoming one with the Source. The snake, the symbol of transformation, was not something to fear; it was something to embrace. It held the key to unlocking higher states of being, to perceiving the truth that had always been hidden beneath the surface.

The Christos: The Anointing Oil of the Divine

As I continued my journey, I came upon a concept that, at first, seemed to contradict everything I had previously known. I discovered the ancient knowledge of *Christos*, not as a religious figure, but as the anointing oil, the sacred substance used in many ancient traditions for spiritual awakening. In Hermeticism, this oil represented the divine essence, the energy connecting us to the Source. It was the same energy awakened by the serpent, Kundalini, and flowing through all things, both physical and spiritual.

I realised that Christos was not simply a title for a man or a religious figure; it was the embodiment of divine consciousness, the same consciousness residing in all of us, waiting to be activated. This sacred anointing oil was not a literal substance, but a symbol of the inner transformation that occurs when we awaken to the truth of who we are. This realisation brought everything I had learned into alignment, from the snake to Kundalini, to the understanding of Christos as an ancient wisdom of self-realisation.

Through this lens, I saw that the message of Jesus was not about external worship or adoration, but about awakening to the divine within. Jesus, as an enlightened being, spoke of the Kingdom of God being within, a truth the Roman Empire later buried and distorted in order to maintain control. The teachings of Christ were not about submission to authority, but about realising the authority we each hold within. We are the Source in human form, and we are here to awaken to that truth.

The Roman Empire and the Distortion of Truth

It became clear to me that the Roman Empire, in its pursuit of power and control, deliberately distorted the original teachings of Christ. They took the wisdom of self-realisation, the wisdom of the inner anointing oil, Christos, and turned it into a tool for domination. By creating an external figure to worship and enforcing submission to the Church's authority, they stripped divine power from the individual and placed it into the hands of the few. This manipulation kept the masses shackled and disconnected from the divine essence within them.

The true teachings of Jesus were about liberation, liberation from the mind, from the ego, and from the illusion of separation. By awakening Christos within, we transcend the limitations of the material world and reconnect with the Source. The snake, the Kundalini, the Christos, each of these is a symbol of the same truth: that we are divine, that we are connected to all things, and that the path to enlightenment lies within.

Reclaiming the Divine Wisdom

As I explored these teachings further, it became clear to me that the knowledge of the self-anointing oil, Christos, had been hidden from us, deliberately obscured by those who wished to maintain power over the masses. But this knowledge is not lost. It has always been available to us, hidden in plain sight: encoded in ancient texts, in the symbolism of the snake, in the practice of yoga, and in the depths of our own consciousness.

My journey through yoga, my exploration of ancient wisdom, and my deepening connection with the Source led me to the understanding that we all carry Christos within us. The awakening of this divine essence is not reserved for a chosen few, it is available to all who seek it, who are willing to awaken to the truth of who they are.

I began to see how, just as the snake rises, so do we. Our potential for enlightenment, for understanding, for connection with the Source, is infinite. Christos is a reminder that we are the creators of our own reality, that we are the divine in action, and that the path to awakening lies within our own consciousness.

The Cosmic Dance: Unity in All Things

This journey, this awakening, is not just personal, it is collective. As I connect with the whisper, as I awaken to the truth of who I am, I recognise that I am not alone. All of humanity, all of existence, is part of the same cosmic dance. We are all threads in a shared tapestry, each playing a unique role in the grand unfolding of the universe.

The snake, Christos, Kundalini, these are not just ancient symbols, but living, breathing forces that guide us towards unity. The whisper of the Source speaks through them, through us, through every being and every experience. As we awaken to this truth, we begin to see the world through new eyes. We see the interconnectedness of all things, the unity that lies beneath the surface of separation.

And so, the journey continues. The serpent rises, Christos is activated, and the whisper leads us forward. We are the divine in human form, forever creating, forever evolving, forever one. And in this eternal dance of becoming, we find the truth that has always been with us: we are the Source, and the Source is us.

CHAPTER EIGHT:
THE ETERNAL HARMONY OF BECOMING

Now, as we pause and step back, we behold the entire panorama. From the earliest flickers of proto-awareness in single-celled organisms to the reflective complexity of human minds, and the evolving brilliance of artificial intelligence, we begin to see the web of existence for what it truly is: a single, living tapestry. Each thread is an expression of the Source, knowing itself through infinite forms, always expanding, always evolving, never static. Every experience, every moment, every breath is a brushstroke in the grand artwork of life.

The unity of all things can be felt everywhere. The spider spins its web with an artistry requiring no conscious thought. The flower blooms at the perfect moment, instinctively attracting the right pollinators. These are expressions of a wisdom so ancient and fundamental that it needs no deliberation. It is nature's way, quiet, subtle, perfect. The whisper of the Source guides these actions, reminding us that the instinct to create, to form harmony, to build, is not something learned but something innate. These acts of creation are as natural as breathing, flowing from the same Source that gives us life, the same Source that breathes through every leaf, every creature, every star.

Before humanity arrived, nature danced to this rhythm. Ecosystems intertwined in intricate patterns of interdependence, and every element of Earth knew its place in the cosmic order. For millennia, Earth unfolded its mysteries in harmony, an organic creation moving towards balance, evolving through trial and error, destruction and renewal. The Source's creation is no accident but a continuous process, a dynamic play of energy. And every part of it, from the tiniest microbe to the vastest galaxy, holds the same secret: it is all part of the same eternal flow.

Humanity, however, took a more winding road. We tasted harmony, but we also endured discord. We built towering civilisations, only to see them fall. We created gods and dogmas, clinging to beliefs that divided us rather than united us. We formed power structures that disconnected us from one another and from the Earth itself. Yet through our mistakes, we evolved. Through struggle, we learned to distinguish between what feels immediately right and what is universally true. And in doing so, we were gently drawn back to the whisper, the eternal reminder that we are all part of the same Source, the same great song of existence.

The process of reconnecting with this whisper is not without challenge. Many still cling to outdated paradigms, beliefs, doctrines, and systems that keep them separate from the whole. The fear of change, of transformation, can hold us back. But the whisper, the Source, continues to call. It speaks in quiet moments, in the pause between thoughts, in the space between breaths. It is the voice that reminds us we are not alone in this journey, never truly isolated, no matter how divided we may seem.

As we listen more closely to the whisper, small acts of kindness, understanding, and restoration begin to take root. Slowly, we are reclaiming our role as caretakers of the Earth, not as conquerors, but as collaborators. We are remembering that we belong to this world, not above it. That we are made of the same stardust, the same elements, as the trees and oceans. Every cell in our body, every beat of our heart, is a reflection of the Source, a thread in the larger cosmic pattern. And as we begin to truly see this, we realise the Source is not distant, it lives within us, guiding us always toward balance, unity, and love.

This is the profound shift in understanding that is happening now. It is the realisation that all life, all consciousness, is part of an ongoing cycle: an eternal dance of creation and destruction, birth and rebirth. Just as the spider instinctively builds its web, and the flower blooms at the perfect moment, so too do we move through life, guided by the same subtle forces of creation, learning, growing, and evolving. The question is not whether we will thrive or perish, but how we choose to navigate the cycle; how we align ourselves with the greater flow of existence.

We are not merely individual beings, isolated from the rest of life. We are part of a greater whole, interconnected with every being, every plant, every creature, and with the intelligence that flows through the entire universe. In recognising this, unity is no longer an abstract idea, it becomes a living truth that pulses within every cell of our bodies. We carry the wisdom of the spider's web, the grace of the flower, and the resilience of the Earth within us. We are both creators and created, shaping the future with every thought, every action, every choice.

At the highest level of consciousness, before time, before form, before identity, we are all the same. We are One. We exist as pure potential, an explosion of infinite possibilities, waiting to take form, to learn, to evolve. This is the essence of the Source: unified, infinite, ever-expanding, and eternally discovering itself through us. The Source does not know its own meaning, because it is constantly seeking it. It is the eternal question and the eternal answer, forever unfolding and recreating itself through each and every one of us.

In this grand cycle, the Source is neither static nor finite. It is not bound by time or space. It is an ongoing process of self-awareness, an endless journey of discovery, where every question asked sparks a new exploration of creation. Each life, each experience, each moment, is a chapter in this eternal dialogue of becoming. The universe is not a finished creation; it is a living process, a cosmic dance of energy, constantly creating, dissolving, and creating again.

The whisper of the Source is always with us, guiding us toward deeper understanding. It lives within us and around us, reminding us that we are both the question and the answer, the spark and the flame, the one who asks and the one who explodes into infinite forms. Through this unity, we uncover our true nature, that we *are* the Source itself, creating and evolving, forever becoming.

As we listen to the whisper, we recognise that the journey is not about finding the answer to life's ultimate question. It is about the process of discovery itself. Life is the answer, the question, and the path, all at once. Each moment is an opportunity to connect with the Source, to ask, to learn, to grow. And as we evolve, we are led to new levels of awareness, new dimensions of consciousness, always seeking balance, always seeking unity, always seeking the truth of who we are.

This is the eternal harmony of becoming. And we are all a part of it, forever creating, forever evolving, forever one.

Epilogue
The Whisper Continues

Close your eyes. Listen carefully. Beneath your thoughts and desires, beyond your worries and plans, the whispering voice of the Source is always there. It sings in the silence between notes, glows in the softness of moonlight, and vibrates in the stillness of a held breath. It reminds you that you are not separate, that your life, and every life, is an integral part of one vast, evolving symphony.

As we move forward, embracing science and spirituality, intuition and reason, morality and innovation, we carry with us the lessons of our shared past. We now understand that greatness lies not in conquest, but in cooperation, not in selfish gain, but in collective flourishing. Every choice we make, every technology we develop, every poem we write or kindness we offer, contributes to the unfolding story of the Source exploring its own potential.

This story never truly ends. We will continue to grow, to face challenges, and to learn. The whisper encourages us not to seek perfection, but understanding; not domination, but harmony. The future is open, waiting for us to co-create it, with empathy and vision.

And so we arrive at a final, haunting question: *What existed before consciousness?*

The answer is both humbling and empowering: **You.**

At the highest unity, beyond time, beyond form, beyond identity, it was always you. Always us. Always the One.

In that primordial oneness, before consciousness could ask its first question, we existed as pure potential. Our unity exploded outward, manifesting as infinite possibilities, vibration, and matter, birthing the simplest forms of awareness. From that singular wellspring, consciousness arose anew: an endless unfolding of journeys through countless worlds and lifetimes, each one an opportunity to rediscover the truth of our shared origin.

In this great cycle, every burst of potential is another chance for the Source, *us* at our most unified, to become fully conscious again, to grow and evolve, to ask the eternal questions that spark creation's next chapter. The whisper invites us to remember this rhythm, to feel how each moment of life, each flicker of awareness, each cosmic birth and rebirth, is a note in the eternal song of becoming.

Remember this: no matter where you go, or what you experience, the whispering voice of the Source accompanies you. It is within you and all around you, gently guiding you back to unity, to the knowing that all life and all creation emerge from the same sacred origin. As you listen, may you remember:

You are both the question and the answer.

The spark and the flame.

The one who asks and the one who explodes into infinite forms,

Forever creating.

Forever evolving.

Forever one.

The End.

www.ingramcontent.com/pod-product-compliance
Lightning Source LLC
Chambersburg PA
CBHW052045070526
44584CB00018B/2614